THE BIGGER PICTURE

THE BIGGER PICTURE

D. A. Prince

HAPPENSTANCE

BY THE SAME AUTHOR:

Bookmarks, Happen*Stance*, 2018
Common Ground, Happen*Stance*, 2014
Nearly the Happy Hour, Happen*Stance*, 2008
Keeping in Touch, Pikestaff, 2002
Without Boundaries, Manifold, 2001
Undoing Time, Pikestaff, 1998

ACKNOWLEDGEMENTS:

Some of these poems, or earlier versions, appeared in the following journals: *Brittle Star, Fenland Poetry Journal, Magma, New Walk, Orbis, Pennine Platform, Prole, Raceme, Seam, Snakeskin, South, Stand, The Fenland Reed, The Frogmore Papers, The High Window, The North, The Rialto*. Some, or earlier versions, appeared in the following anthologies: *Birdbook: Saltwater and Shore* (ed. Kirsten Irving and Jon Stone) 2016, *Ware Competition Anthology* (2018), *Wondering Soul* (in response to the Methodist Art Collection), 2019. 'Musée des Beaux Chapeaux' was commissioned for the installation *No Rhyme Nor Reason*, StAnza 2021. Four poems were previously included in *Bookmarks* (Happen*Stance*, 2018) and 'The Window' was highly commended in *The Forward Book of Poetry 2020*.

NOTE FOR VISUALLY IMPAIRED READERS:

The jacket features a wallpaper-style background of large green skeleton leaf shapes against a paler green and white background. The title is centred in the middle of the front jacket in large dark green caps, one word per line, with the author's name below in smaller lower case. The back jacket has a pale green oblong area with some descriptive text, followed by an endorsement quote and then the whole text of the poem 'Two Plants' (also on page 61).

First published in 2022 by Happen*Stance* Press
21 Hatton Green, Glenrothes KY7 4SD
https://happenstancepress.com

ISBN: 978-1-910131-70-1

All rights reserved

Poems © D. A. Prince, 2022

The right of D. A. Prince to be identified
as author of this work has been asserted in accordance
with the Copyright, Designs & Patent Act, 1988

Printed & bound by Imprint Digital, Exeter
https://digital.imprint.co.uk

CONTENTS

The Future / 9
Visibility / 10
The Ticket to the Museum of Time / 11
The Viewing Point / 12
History Lessons / 14
One Side of History / 15
Neighbouring / 16
Illegal / 17
The Traveller / 18
Heading for Tirana / 19
Musée des Beaux Chapeaux / 20
The Stolen Shadow / 21
Silence / 22
The Raising of Lazarus / 23
The Mass of St Hubert / 24
Students in the Courtauld / 25
Iggy Pop Life Class, 2016 / 26
The House of Cards / 28
'Is Your Journey Really Necessary?' / 30
The Selmer Series VI Saxophone (1954–74) / 31
'Prometheus Unbound' / 32
No Worse / 33
Might Have Been / 34
Truth / 35
Reconstruction / 36
All There Was to Do / 37
Fahrkarte Europa / 38
Hotel Schwann / 39
The Architect's Couple / 40
The Artist's Impression / 41
Sabbioneta / 42
Le Vieux Port, Marseille / 43
Hotel Europa / 44
Billet à Composter / 45
Into April / 46

Homesick / 47
Distraction / 48
Rock Pipit / 49
3.00 a.m. / 50
The Window / 52
The Knife / 53
Holding the Camera / 54
Her Voice / 55
'A Matter of Life and Death' / 56
'L'Éclisse' / 57
Shot in Academy Ratio / 58
'If I've Got to Remember' / 59
The Painter of Icons / 60
Two Plants / 61
Into the Solstice / 62
Petition / 63
Stones / 64
A Trick or the Light / 65
'Consumir preferente antes del fin de:' / 66
Shopping List / 67
The Four Old Things / 68
The Prize-Winning Mathematical Theory / 70

About the Author / 73

for David

THE FUTURE

'...their idiotic human faith in the future'
   —Camus, *The Plague*

What I love most is its salt distance,
blue and cloudless, its compass needle
fixed to the light—a light both clear
and deceiving, and North never as true
as we're told. Yet we believe, the way belief
is a cradle no one outgrows, placing it
somewhere near the sea's horizon. How
it draws the eye, leaves space for levelled questions,
for the blips of ships pricking the sky
before they vanish. How it shimmers, out there,
a beyond we can't measure, out of time,
erasing the words we pin on calendars. How
out of reach it is; how it could be anywhere,
unfathomed, immaterial. How it's not here.

VISIBILITY

In some lights you can see them clearly—
those wind-farm masts, far out, in a line
like silver stubble pricking the horizon.

With the sea flat-calm, in some lights
they come so close you could zip your coat
and walk out, salt-road-easy.

Their arms are siren-welcome, with an unheard song
that in some lights rings like a summer shower
on shingle, clean as a rinsed moon.

You've studied direction, where to stand, undazzled,
linking eyes; you also know in some lights
they refuse even an outline, leaving the sky empty.

Days when they're invisible, when the rough fetch
gnaws at the beach, chews the cliffs with worry,
in some lights changing the places of earth and sky

you hunker down, try not to read answers
in rain-ribs hurrying down the glass,
trusting you'll still see clearly in some lights.

THE TICKET TO THE MUSEUM OF TIME

Let's be honest, it was raining.
Besançon's citadel needed clearer skies,
more sun. But this museum was open.
That's why we went in.

Five euros paid the gatekeeper, and if
the children shriek and if the teachers sigh
it could be our own past we hear,
not this *école*, wide-mouthed at Foucault's pendulum.

Upstairs the floorboards creak, telling today
the ways of watch springs, hour glasses,
minute hands. Museum stuff: the calendars
of saints and feasting, anniversaries;

the almanacs with phases of the moon;
the tides and market days. In the vitrines
lie lives and diaries, and in the rooms
the ticking and the ticking off of clocks.

How minutes, hours, centuries are stored—
so many ways to label passing time,
so much memento mori. The *écoliers*
don't come up here, although their voices carry.

The ticket's (too long in my pocket) damp,
ruckled, and though the date's too blurred to read
it's pressed inside this book, holding the place
the future will come back to, given time.

THE VIEWING POINT

Past the repeated *Danger* signs and ten-foot fence
topped with barbed wire, between the stubby trees
choked with some shreds of plastic rabbit-guards,
close where the path, puddled but passable, divides;

up, leaving the older oaks and gangly ash,
dodging some snagging brambles, last year's berries
no more than knots, careful on stones sucked loose
in a path half-watercourse in winter;

swerving past outcrops, stubborn bedrock flecked
with mosses, climbing through shallow-rooted rowan
and struggling sycamore, eyes down and glancing
left, right, and just a yard ahead, no more—

to flattened ground. An information board
half-legible under its fog of lichen.
Geology. The facts of granite chippings,
sponsors and history. This promised view.

*

Who thought the trees could grow like this?
Would grow like *trees*? Would cluster till
the only view's its own tight circle
ringed with curtaining birch? Down there

should be the landmarks—smudged and smoky town,
school roof and cemetery, heavy clay
and playing fields, the geography of when
this quarry-edge was newly-cut, and sharp

with menace and the daily blasts. Instead
a living screen of this year's leaves,
and sunlight picking out the grasses,
new-season itching at the edge

as though the climb could only ever
end up here—inward, and centred
wholly in a cradling hum of bees,
a brief and welcome emptiness.

HISTORY LESSONS

Peace had no dates—it sprawled
shapeless in gaps between the wars,
dragging its chapters into emptiness.
Foreign relations rearranged the maps
in black and grey, and tired constitutions tried
to understand themselves, while twice a day
the quarry shook our windows, coughing dust
as white as blackboard chalk. Under the town
black seams were emptied, and their coal was drawn
until the pavements buckled. In the classroom
a lesson crawled across a hundred years.
A textbook page could hold five decades
curled in its corners, blurring to the space
contained between the end-of-lesson bells.

So it was war, staking out the centuries,
holding it all together, that got us through
exams—the dates of Jenkins' Ear, or the long trail
across the Peninsula.
Time bullied through whole chapters
and all the maps turned red. Wars made sense,
each with a list of causes to tick off,
linking the battles. The Lines of Torres Vedras
were inked across our notes, and armies
arrowed across the shrunken continent
to win in half a sentence. Lesson over,
scraping back chairs, we packed
the foreign names of victory
into the scuff of satchels. Done.

ONE SIDE OF HISTORY

We learned. They were foreign,
dark-deeded, defined by dates,
coughing up vowels stinking of garlic,
dead in their plots of obfuscation.

We took O-levels
in their single-minded hatred,
their campaigns and devious marriages.
We were made to re-draw maps
and wrote essays on legitimacy of heirs
and family trees. We copied lists
of what were called 'religious practices'.

We spelled them properly,
marvelling at their mismatched consonants,
summed them up
in paragraphed half-pages,
pinned them to neat headings,
underlined their weaknesses.

They were not, we learned,
like us.
Never like us.

NEIGHBOURING

Night brings their voices closer, as though
over water, with ripples of laughter,
glass-clink, moths batting at our lamps
and the hedge of separation disappearing and dissolving.
Shared air crackles with star-bursts of sound, un-worded
in mutual darkness, a rattle of something raucous,
untroubled by hawthorn, bramble, holly
and all the legal boundaries homes have.

Too dark ever to recognise them, this family
living loud, beyond our edge. Even the trees
have vanished into midnight and the sky.
Darkness is all and only sound
and thick with questions. In tomorrow's daylight
we can never know them near as this.

ILLEGAL

Slipped across the border, keeping tight indoors,
locks on your tongue, never a gap
in closed curtains, one ear tuned
to the elsewhere of neighbours, the street,
the traveller who could still
knock on the moonlit door
                             the pause
before snapping the padlock of silence,
first step on new-laid ice, testing the trap
set by surprise, the opening of proverbs,
the trip of unmatched endings
                             living
with the volume up, jamming the airways,
stuffing each crack with paper, loading
the dice in your own favour, knowing
how your words danced in daylight, once.

THE TRAVELLER

Someone said *map* but he wanted none of that
with its borders and queasy negotiation
drawn tight, all steel wires and razored edges
and need to be understood. Any direction
was rough and enough to unhitch him,
leaving his shadow to bleach by the ditch
and his footprints dissolving in sand.

So he listened: to the wind, the grit in the grass,
an invisible bird seeking water, voices
from star after star after star, and re-discovered
old magnetic ways deep in the earth.
He lost the language of phones and fear.
Love was the last to go, its goodbye
salting his heart and hands.

He was so far ahead he vanished
into the clutch of night, winter, whatever
lay there waiting and watchful, ever watchful;
into the press of paper and print, the push
of by-laws and more; into the regulation
of spaces, places of *can* and *can't* and cant,
and then state and street and straight

and what he was free of and for and why,
where the eternal questions return
in the gaudy disguise of new gods. If someone
had ever said *myth* he'd have spurned that too,
alone on his only road, walking out and away
and unwritten, sure from his side
there is no other ground for an answer.

HEADING FOR TIRANA

Though the state rolls its tarmac straight
out of town, heading for the capital,
the job's only half-done. Glance sideways
between houses squatting in their dust
and the roads crumble to gravel.
Two car-lengths in and they're back
to the age of cart ruts and pot holes.

This road ignores them, working along a vein
of new-build offices, half-built, punched through
with gaps where windows might go. Someday
they'll ripen into frames, their polished glass
matching their pillared porticos. Someone
has plans for cabling and computers,
the future's office furniture. Somehow.

Today their flights of stairs go nowhere,
end mid-air. Fifteen feet up—
too high for chance—one has a rope of garlic
swinging in the draught. On the bend
another wears a ram's skull,
the ridged coils of its horns wedged
in a tangle of rusty rebar.

Ask, then. The answer's wrapped up in a shrug,
a look-away, that old response to change—
for luck, perhaps, or to avert the evil eye.
The skull's rage glares from empty sockets.
The garlic's rotted in the rain. And the guide,
eager to show his country's roots, explains
Yes, they will hang anything. Anything, really.

MUSÉE DES BEAUX CHAPEAUX

After W.H. Auden and Edward Lear

About head-coverings he was never wrong,
the Quangle-Wangle: how capaciously they demonstrate
be-ribboned status; how they conceal
the extent of loneliness even within the false comforts
of gratified indulgence; how their expanse
is an island where in the ordinary way of things
life goes privately and inevitably on.

In the Crumpetty Tree, however, how the ones and twos,
tentative on their individual and idiosyncratic journeys,
enlarge his whole society, flocking to his hat-shaped space
and multitude of welcomes; how the possibilities
of home and settlement bring them singing together
the notes of their native tunes; how it's something and amazing,
having somewhere to come to, wherever they had come from.

THE STOLEN SHADOW

A cold tale, even in translation.
It ends with his body, shuttered, four friends
stumbling at the corners, twisting
his emptiness over cart ruts, roots,
the road too far off, the saving hope
shrivelling past thistles, teasels, seed-heads
gone brittle. Husks. Before that, his last cry
like a rusty hinge or a blackbird
pinned by a hawk, the knowledge
tearing his throat till his voice-cords frayed.
The wall trembled and held its ground,
too late, too settled, its joints too closed,
and silenced to shift. The mallet clunked
and fell from his fingers. There was a clink
like a dead bell. Before that—just before—
he'd looked up, caught the sun's eye,
felt a flush spring in his cheeks,
thought of a future, his shadow swinging
along the ground, that hole, the foundation stone
waiting, his shadow still making playthings
out of the mason's hands, teasing the light
and lightness over that gap, the trap
for the first stone. Until the stone snared him,
the mason cunning, knowing a shadow
gives strength to the build, and his own under the wall,
leaving him no longer himself. Before that,
he'd known vigilance, not letting his shadow
out of his sight, his mother's warning
packing him off for the day, the bite
of morning frost, one boot leaking, and waiting
for time to mend it. Before that, the moon
still up, and his shadow crisp on the silver earth
as much a part of him as breath,
as the life he was birthed to, before that.

SILENCE

So you go back to the hills, this time
for the good, for the presence
that sings the clear bowl of sky with the same
pure notes of nothing. Not absence
(not now) but the unclouded colour
of harebell, that crystalline glitter of quartz
veined in the rock, the way a collar
of water waits in yesterday's hoof-prints,
the wordless felt of fine grass. The air
is a hair's-breadth below a whisper,
barely breathing, tuned to attention where
shadows arrange their own version of vespers
for the settling sun. It's all you've wished for:
this gift of learning how the world turns,
how the power of silence makes it more.

THE RAISING OF LAZARUS

You wonder, don't you, what they said
afterwards—neighbours, people from his street
who'd never seen the like. *Beyond belief,*
perhaps, shaking their heads. *I couldn't
believe my eyes.* When they talked later
(witnesses, late-comers trying to make sense of it)
patching together versions, what had they seen?
Death and his sisters' grief,
the rites of being laid to rest.
The tomb's finality.
                          Then
nothing that tallied: cross-talk, argument.
Everything they couldn't have seen, but did.
How slowly he got up, finding his feet—
Well, you'd be stiff—four days down there!
What of that friend who called him back to life?

And as for Lazarus, returned to breath,
gulping and blinking, shaking off the cloths,
warmed into feeling, what did he see
in the changed world he'd left?
Perhaps the sunlight blazed too bright
for comprehension, his senses shrinking
from this newly-sharpened world
of screaming colour. Or looking round—
bewildered faces and a hum of doubt—
did he leave all the questioning to them?

THE MASS OF ST HUBERT

Workshop of the Master of the Life of the Virgin, 1485-90
  —National Gallery, London

Even at Mass, at the altar step,
there's a dog, taking no notice of
the angel fluttering down with a stole,
keen to adorn the future St Hubert. Acolytes
quiver, perking up for the unexpected
but the dog—ash-coloured, quietly crouched,
deep in his own contemplation
of inner canine bliss—ignores
this ethereal lack-of-smell, this soundless
shift of air. Accustomed to fidgeting
and rustlings, the wordless ways of lesser priests,
he holds his own attention to the stones,
a sniff of swept dust, a footprint's invisible trace.
He senses all the mumbling passing hours,
the seasons with their colours; knows indifference.
He is constancy, and untroubled.
He was never the hound who hunted stags.
Whatever sainthood will happen beyond
this consecration, he will remain
the grey detail, central, an anchor, at rest,
a small part of the bigger picture.

STUDENTS IN THE COURTAULD

Checking their phones, breaking off
to text or laugh or share the latest tweet,
what they miss is this: the concentrated need
for work and working, the desperate fear
Soutine knows in each face, the hungry holding-on
to uniform and hard-earned title.

Take *The Little Pastry Cook*, his whites so large
his body barely touches this cocoon
of stiffened cotton, too large for his years.
All nerves and ears, you'd think he hardly dares
to sleep or fold inside himself, his life
a taut perfection of a fragile art. He's
one of those airy creations Soutine leaves
to float unseen between the canvas
and our inner eyes.
                    All these students see
is brushwork gawkiness and his scrawny neck
filling the time before—a latte?
cappuccino?—folders closing tight
and crayons zipped away, all easy smiles
and solid confidence. Years ahead,
chancing upon their notebooks, packed away,
how will they read this unfamiliar face,
this broken sketch of someone out of reach?

IGGY POP LIFE CLASS, 2016

An exhibition of 53 drawings by 22 artists with Iggy Pop as model
 —Brooklyn Museum Collection, curated by Jeremy Deller

i.

How they talked him
into four hours of stillness
no one recorded
but every fold of skin
holds, for a moment, something
of monument and godhead.

Even the group photo—all twenty-two artists
gathered in synchronised glow—
has him naked, tanned, central,
the only fig-leaf a carefully-sited student.

ii.

Where you stand, the angle you take,
pencil listening for any clue:

for some it has to be a portrait,
where below the neck's creased concertina
the body is abandoned
to reverent imagination.

iii.

It's a revelation, how buttocks pleat
against a hard plinth.
Then, how the penis is blurred.

iv.

Sharp as steel, the pencil's point in the right hands
can score every shadow, taking time
back through the greys of observed formality
to the unpersoned page, where
the body's surface, however criss-crossed
with years and weather, speaks
beyond itself of the spirit. Twenty-two pencils
are witness to the truth.

THE HOUSE OF CARDS

After Jean-Siméon Chardin's *The House of Cards*, 1735,
the first of Chardin's four paintings of this subject
   —Waddesdon Manor, National Trust

A boy is building a house of cards.
It should be simple. All he needs—
the pack, table, chair, some light
and air to hold them. A servant, perhaps,
neat in the grey-brown livery that suits
the habit of Chardin's palette.

A balanced moment and nothing falling
except daylight across green baize,
touching the boy's face with a soft brush
of concentration. Silence visible.
No movement in the air or his hands
holding the Ace of Hearts, poised

for risk, his breath caught, for ever.
Framed, leaning forward to his house,
this single storey, he is readying himself
for the one move that might undo it all.
Time hangs in the curtains' folds.
The King of Clubs leers from a yawning drawer

and the future waits to be told.
In one room, muted and viewless,
his eyes drawn to the fingered edge of the card,
freed from whatever duties lie beyond,
while the oil dries on the canvas
a boy is building a house of cards.

      *

It should be simple. Cards, a table—
the essentials—and a boy (not yet a man).
Nothing beyond the wooden frame,
no little landscape glimpsed through a window.
No servant girl pausing to pout in a half-open door—
the sort of showing-off a painter brings
to pack a scene or titillate.
It should be finished now, this house of air,
but Chardin can't leave. Today
he'll close the door but won't let go
cards, a table, and the boy.
And what of the air?

*

The essentials. Chardin returns three times
re-arranging a boy, a table, and the cards.
Three more pictures. Not the same boy.
Do they matter so much, those props,
these materials he keeps working at
under his brush? Are the new cards
more anxious, more inclined
to risk and what might fall? A sweeping hand
or collapsed by chance: all one in the end.
But we never see the end, only this.
A painter fretting at the tipping point of fate
and a boy, building a house of cards.

'IS YOUR JOURNEY REALLY NECESSARY?'

Too light too soon. Listening as whiteness
leaks round the curtain edge
we know excuse has drifted in with sleep.
While one cold hand fumbles for the radio—
lists of blocked roads, closed schools—
we can unwrite the diary of today.

Look! a white cap, five inches high, makes a chef
of the lamp post. Yesterday's paths have vanished
and the garden no longer knows itself,
snuggled in the smoothed white of its duvet.
What can we do but stay indoors, peeping out
to muffled figures that were trees?

Snow makes us draw breath. For just one day
being irrelevant to the humming world
is not so hard. Unhooked from travelling,
lit by the shine from window-sills piled white,
we're back in childhood, with an absence note
and the snow's smile of glittering alibi.

THE SELMER SERIES VI SAXOPHONE (1954–74)

'Selmer's General Manager Jerome Selmer has confirmed that all Mark VIs were manufactured from industry-standard 66/34 'yellow brass' stock and that Selmer never recycled shell casings.'
 —Wikipedia

It was a good story: those early instruments
recycling unused war, lifting music
out of shell casings and scrap artillery,
and all that stuff of slaughter melted down,
cleansed of its guilt, changed
into the shining currency of the New Age.

A story for its time. Success, refashioned,
gleaming and wrapped like gold around the notes.
Something that re-imagines years of waste, re-makes
brute metal, sparks the furnaces, renews
those elements. A shining singing line
to show where the polish comes from.

Like any story (as though *good* and *true*
aren't slippery as ice) it lets need
play to the legend. If a tune can float—
various and sly and looping—let it lie
loose on the air, lightness and laughter in its breath.
And what else *is* a story, after all?

'PROMETHEUS UNBOUND'

I could swear, on oath, I've never read this play,
ignorance my alibi, though I'd plead guilty
to all the dazzled hours spent with 'Adonais', even quote
whole stanzas (that 'white radiance of eternity')
from this Oxford Standard Authors heavyweight.

Shelved, Shelley stands tallest (so, *un*-Standard, then?)
towering a good inch over Wordsworth. The same blue,
the same tiredness along the spine,
stiffened with lack of interest. Untouched, unopened since;
just one more casualty on the tracks of time.

But look! A fine black ball-point's underscored
the fiery argument. My student hand
has shrunk to footnotes—shamed
in pedantry and this precise absurdity—
all Shelley's raging against tyranny.

What did I dare to think I knew, back then,
in that summer of love, when Sgt. Pepper
spun on every turntable, when Paris
tore its streets up, when the news
crackled through shared transistor radios?

NO WORSE

Silence stretches a hundred miles
between our clenched phones.
But nothing was broken, she says. Then
It could have been worse.

Silence develops the other story
while we stuff its throat with clatter
of next week, books, a trip to London
and back. *He's fine now*, she says. *Really.*

Silence, off stage, waits for a cue.
He bled for two hours, she adds, then
switches to *The Archers,* where its plot might go,
and could I not ring while it's on.

Silence cuts in. *The other bloke*, she says,
didn't hang around after. The shwa-shwa of traffic
then and now, our eyes hearing only that road
and no one stopping, no one at all.

But nothing was broken, she says again.
It could have been worse. Silence listens,
stores it all up for the small hours.

MIGHT HAVE BEEN

He wrote himself the obituary he would like,
striking out real parents and closed gritty streets. Instead
he sketched a smallholder, slight and silvery,
whose guinea fowl won prizes in East Anglian county shows
and a mother whose children's books brought some success.
This pleased him. And them, he decided, catching for a moment
imagined faded faces, touched with their own excellence.
He'd always liked the country, so he wrote them all
a house within sight of the sea in winter
(though eager hedges packed with nests and song
shrank the summer view, just like a story).
He gave himself a sister. Two sisters. More confident,
the canvas began to fill and acquire perspective.
He let one die young. The epidemic (his mother was never the same).
He stuck then, trying to picture a face, give her a name.
'Ellie', he decided, after a TV star. His other sister, older by twelve months,
was dark-eyed, moody, danced. Became theatrical
(she'd run away from home) and played the pier-end shows
with Pantomime in Manchester most years.
He'd been the clever one—and that seemed right—
grammar school, university (London, he thought, and Ancient History).
He couldn't see himself in sciences. Or the Army.
He couldn't see himself in anything. Growing up
had often been a problem.
Perhaps he'd die young, too. That was always easier
or would have been if he hadn't lived on,
the life he'd never wanted holding him back.

TRUTH

Worked over by philosophers
until the rubbed surface is free,
closer to a sea-worn pebble
sanded smooth by relentless tides

like the one lingering deep
in a jacket pocket
when summer's over—the one
you picked up, couldn't throw away,
the one your hand returns to.

RECONSTRUCTION

So far, so true: we came to the island
and found the column, or it found us
as landmarks do, two hundred feet of it
making us doll-sized. Out of a landscape—
hardly hills, more like a flattened spread of fields
pegged down and reaching for the sea—
it lorded history. Above our heads
the sky snagged on the Great Man's epaulettes,
his sword. We'd seen a postcard, read the facts
of dates and victories, the opening times,
how many steps, no unaccompanied children,
how much (in shillings). There was a door, I'm sure.

And then? That door, wooden and tired with too much sun;
its handle, and my hand. This hand,
and nothing more. And if we paid, and trod
each of the hundred and fifteen steps, stopping
for breath, and going on, circling
higher, higher, that's how it would have been,
and the view only another postcard
fading and playing tricks with memory.
And if we did, how would I know the truth
and not what could have been
imagination doing its work? One staircase curls
much like another, until the fumbled hand-rail
and the too-tight door, shuffling into light
and a wrenching wind. Who's there to ask?

ALL THERE WAS TO DO

Take turns, leaping out, to open each gate
and drag it tight-shut behind the car.

Pull sheeps' wool from rusting wire
competing for the fattest bundles.

Build dams from stones and rushes
across the icy headlong of a stream.

Be brave across the slatted bridge, water
too visible, the only way to the farm.

Sit quietly at table, waiting for crusts
to throw to the dozen yellow-fanged dogs.

Dabble in the river, fast and shallow,
hurrying down through summer;

fish for trout. Pick red currants,
scratch the hard bright flea bites,

go to bed by candle light. Dream
in the rapid language of the river.

FAHRKARTE EUROPA

Nineteen-euros-worth of second-class scene-change
(*von Ljubljana nach Nove Gorica*)
through the melting greens of wood and meadow
and glimpses of water, and this ticket
stamped '06' twice over, so we changed—where?

In yesterday's rain the echoing museum had taught us
'nine types of Slovenian hay rack' but not
how to map the valleys. So we missed
the mixed alphabet of letters naming the where,
remembering instead a guard
surprised by our journey, anxious
not to be responsible, steering us onward,
edgewards. We had other connections, lists,
a border we had to reach,
part of a passage out, an unlikely transience.

Now there's only this ticket, reused in a book,
to mark the slip from one country to the next
and, somewhere in the middle, a change.

HOTEL SCHWANN

Busy setting out cold meats, pumpernickel,
sliced cheeses on the mixed florals of old china,
transforming the *Weinstube* (closed indefinitely)
into a breakfast room, they hide even from themselves
how this must be their last season.

His English is good and careful, explaining
the small dog's paw (bandaged) and where to find the key.
But they are never out. Afternoons,
they sit in the *Weinstube* (closed indefinitely)
with *Der Spiegel*'s small print and letters from their son.

When he presents the bill (four nights,
meticulous in fountain pen) we have
the courtesies of cash, and his relief. He hopes
we loved his city, as did Goethe; yes, alas,
the *Weinstube* will be closed indefinitely.

THE ARCHITECT'S COUPLE

Their plates are croissant-crumbed, and now she's bored
with sitting on this balcony, coffee
grown cold and the metal chairs harder.

She would have added cushions but the brief
was steel/glass/minimal (*'your perfect life'*)
and every polished surface sharply drawn.

If she leans on the rail, leaving her partner
browsing a blank screen, the wind twists her hair
hissing 'carefree' and 'easy', and her bones

ache in the chill funnelled between high-rise
and the river. She thinks: coat, a knot of scarves,
wool. Not a fluttery shirt hinting at see-through.

The twiggy trees below will never grow leaves
enough to make litter. Later, as per contract,
they must stroll improbably long-legged

among others, their kind, cool and shadowless.
It won't rain. The brief insists on sunlight, stippled
with all the confidence of settled weather.

THE ARTIST'S IMPRESSION

We try our best but his vision of perfection
demands so much. Sometimes we forget
to stroll hand in hand, looking about us
with elongated longing, slim as city trees
 and with their same light movement.
We neglect the stretching of our necks, to float
on a faint smudge of shadow
cross-hatched round our feet. Not that we reject
this cleansed and stately vision of us—how
his computer has enhanced us, where
it never rains and no one wears a coat.
Here it is always early evening, spring;
white wine ahead, a serving of small talk.
He trusts us to perform in malls, piazzas,
places where promise gleams like polished glass
and sells the future as an ever-rising share.
When we lose the graceful hang of this,
swapping performance for the back streets
with their chips and deep-fried relishing,
he drags us back, forcing
more steel into our spines. We try our best
behind our pale and unreflecting masks.

SABBIONETA

Città ideale, reached
from a guide book's footnote,
two trains and a lazy bus
way beyond Mantua,
trusting in timetables.

Hazy light of harvest
spreading its gritty dust.
Levelled fields Virgil
would recognise, the order
of gridded streets.

Plum tomatoes, lorry-loads,
a trail of rich-red ripeness,
the day's work done.
Who wouldn't want to live there?

LE VIEUX PORT, MARSEILLE

Dawn slips a thin knife down the shutter's edge
straight as a plumb-line, sharp and quickening.
Morning, with the mistral pleading
and moaning at the warped frames,
is too full of shining view and glitter
of lined-up yachts with their singing halyards,
the jostle of crowded ferries, unloaded workers
running, like the *Edmond Dantès*, to timetables.

It's all too bright, this slap of full sun
hitting the water, throwing its blaze along the quay,
heating it up like a grill. Already
one boat's settled in, selling its catch. A woman
heaves the dead weight of a tuna to her stall.
There's blood and tourists and their cameras—
too much to look at. The piled-up roofs,
a tower (all that's left of a church), the fort
in rose-tinted restoration: later explorations.

In the hindsight of home, too far north
and inland in curtained dark, the memory revives—
the shutters, their sliced light, the singing wind,
heat and the welcomed sunburst of the dazzling day.

HOTEL EUROPA

Signed down a side street, back street, somewhere
in any city, where the ting and rattle
of a typewriter wouldn't be out of place
and only languages have family,
here's where the loose ends come together,
joining scraps of wandering stories
into patchwork, warm and coffee-stained,
when mass bells mark out squares and hours.

A building that wears shared loneliness, the old loden
outlasting its owner. Under the counter
a stack of letters, too late, find a last home
as though the present hasn't happened.
That could be Joseph Roth sitting with his glass,
scribbling the city before the night train leaves.

BILLET À COMPOSTER

Chartres to Illiers-Combray, searching
the same lost time (as though we ever could)
and *Swann's Way* marked exactly where pink hawthorn
burst into rosette flower, fizzing crimson
colouring the calendar, humming with holiday,
throbbing sweet and scented and ordained;
to imagine grandfather, calling out
the gruffest kindness, seeing in the young Marcel
a shared delight; Sunday's unbuttonedness.

Our Saturday, mid-May, the two-coach TER on time,
and spires breaking the skyline beyond fields,
measuring the distances against the clock.
Walking from the station, passing villas
and sprawling gardens, one of many days
tracing the handwriting of smaller towns, until
the pinprick recognition: that's the church,
the gate Swann used, Tante Leonie's,
the baker selling madeleines,

and the hawthorn, bold and arching,
the lane a maze of chapels, and the sun
patterning the ground with windows.
A strident cuckoo and his childhood call—
all here, marked as by accident.
Give my love to the pink hawthorn
wrote a friend in Rome. We do, in triplicate.

INTO APRIL

The primroses have never been better—
and though we say this every year
each year it's true. This month, under skies
released from chains of vapour trails,
they gleam sharp in an unexpected frost.
Afternoon light softens them to silk,
then evening sees them bright below the hedge.
As though they know our need
for something like comfort, something
lying outside ourselves; as though
the natural world is answering a prayer.

Every year a new awakening—
dark holly's polished leaves,
a hawthorn's cheeky brilliant green,
the nearly-bursting buds crowding the cherry,
the air oblivious to human fear
and sunlight's magnificent indifference.

HOMESICK

—for wood sorrel of all things, close up,
and its shy whiteness threaded
with purple veins, still and downcast,
away from the sun's glare,
in shadows where winter lingers late

—for the green lettering of its leaves,
their creased precision soft as fresh paint,
and even in the mind an untrodden green
so splinter-sharp it cut this morning walk
clean from its passing traffic and the dust

—for where it grew, for the nameless paths
stalked and stumbled through and played in;
for the way it returned, each spring,
its own alleluia, in such places
where it flowered brilliant and fragile and again.

DISTRACTION

(http://leicesterperegrines.org.uk/camera-one/)

Too easy when one click opens the webcam
on their world above the city. Even
when the peregrines are absent there's a glimpse
of half a street, sometimes a walker.
Sometimes two. Their weather five miles off
is seen, not heard, and treeless; no thin branches
signalling distress. When there's a feather, fluttering
in their gravel scrape, the wind's an easterly.
Today a camera-smudge of someone's thumb.
This morning's ice lifts off from city roofs.

What I should be doing isn't this. But other lives—
even these birds, that lonely jogger, tiles
defrosting themselves—even on screen
are ways of staying in touch. The peregrines
(a he and she, but not last year's) are bonding.
He's her first-time mate while she's his third
this season; females clawing, killing for him.
Sometimes you never know their story's end;
it goes off-camera, into guess-work, blood.
And what I should be doing isn't this.

ROCK PIPIT

Sea lark, the old men called it, rock lark,
for want of something better,
this bird whose *fit-fit*
has nothing soaring in its notes
nor any song to speak of,
only this flickering head-down brown
and tail-wag purpose between
salt-crust and driftwood and the jetsam
from ferries below its low horizon.

Here, rock-picking, it hides
under the habit of surviving, attending
only to tidelines and routines,
shore space and what water brings,
being almost anonymous, fitting in
among unnamed scraps of roughly land,
along these deckle edges. We, knowing little,
would call it inhospitable. The rock pipit
calls it home.

3.00 A.M.

The Welsh legislation specifically states that 'No person living outside Wales may enter or remain in Wales without a reasonable excuse'
   —*Manchester Evening News*, 06/11/20

The radio fills with closed roads, police checks
at the border and orders to stay local.
At 3.00 a.m.—and every hour of restless questions—
the only route is through recall,
remembering the best of how it was.
               Tonight, that cliff path. Not the climb,
not up the loose slate, shale and polished rock,
the only hand-grab a blood-red snatch
of rotting wire, not the rasping breath
of gradient and watching every step.
None of that.
               Tonight will be
the high and breezy cliff-top,
grass rubbed down to nearly-nothing in the wind,
open to all-round view—from grey roofs, sprawl
of town and factories, and then inland
to lonely farms and dots of working lives,
to north and south and overlap of hills
holding this coast. And the enormous sea
alive with hectic light, the waves whipped up
to spit and spray, their arguments with cliffs
lost in the rattling air.
               Tonight will be
the far-side path, downward, one-walker-wide,
channelled by rain's familiarity,
between the dizzying drop (our left) and (right)
a bank with bracken, bramble, violets,
topped with wool-snaggled wire
and urgent bleating lambs; with crows, with gulls,
with salt breathed in at every sunlit stile.

Down, past the tangled pines, the broken relics
of winter storms, old branches heaped, unreachable;
down, towards the scoop of beach, rock-pools,
a baby river trickling through the sand;
down to its creaking bridge, the flat of roads
and caravans' exotic names and crazy golf
and carpark grids.
               Tonight—again, again—
re-winding the loose-limbed insouciance
we took for granted once, how much.

THE WINDOW

That was my first job, he said, as we gazed
at the insignificant window. Down
the slate steps, and looking from the raised
salt-pitted pavement, where this end of town
gets hammered by the sea, it looked so small.
But sturdy, strongly-made enough to prove
that here his father fitted him with all
the craftsmanship he'd need. It wouldn't move
or crumble. Each year he'd return, to see
his work enduring. Then brought me, to know
a detail of our family history
and let this shabby mullioned window show
something inherited—that stone and wood,
well-built, can last a lifetime and go on
drawing the clean light in and doing good.
I think about it often now he's gone.

THE KNIFE

Other people's knives—they never fit
the way this paring knife sits in my hand,
finding its place. No pedigree (free gift
with something half a century ago).
Death dates it, and the skill of sharpening knives
died with him. That last time (and unaware
his days were shortening) he gave the blade
an edge that's never dulled, that's always keen
to slice a windfall apple or dig round
a wound gouged dark in the potato's side.
Its criss-cross scratches catch the kitchen light.
They could be yesterday's, and fresh and clean
and part of every meal. Nothing remarkable—
except it is: this ordinariness.

HOLDING THE CAMERA

More grey than black and white, four faces
smile straight into the lens, and a horse
(in profile) looks away. No date,
no pencilled names. Everyone knew
who they were, and where, and when
and always would. Their moment,
captured, lasts for ever. Together
and across the miles,
sharing the photograph you've scanned,
we re-assemble names, three faces spoken for.

But not the child.
The girl who dares us to reply.
The dates we push at her don't fit.

Her confidence beams back—sure of her place—
into the eyes behind the camera,
those unknown steadied hands, who see
her image upside down, small as a thumbnail.
Would she remember—stopped from being who she is
and fixed in fading acetate—holding her breath
and smiling till the shutter clicked?
You think she would; you want her name
dovetailed within your version of the past.

I want to know who stands behind the lens.

HER VOICE

Not that I listened much, back then, or thought
I did. *In one ear and out the other*
was what she'd say, before the side door slammed
and I was out, running late, racing through—

what? I'd left her words and warnings caught
between the ironing board and clothes horse, over
the fire guard. Not that I'd ever jammed
my fingers in my ears, sworn at her view

but so much future beckoned; life looked short
and urgent. Nothing she'd know, my mother,
or so it seemed. My hours must be crammed
not trapped indoors. But she's the one who

speaking my name, just that, still shakes me out
of dreams, breathless, unsure whether
I'm back or she is, with her eyes un-filmed,
or where on earth or elsewhere we've come to.

'A MATTER OF LIFE AND DEATH'

—Directed by Michael Powell and Emeric Pressburger, 1946. UK

Digitally restored—and none of its gentleness lost—
another generation surrenders to the screen
where Heaven's comforting bureaucracy is no more
than daily invoices matched to delivery dates.
Desk clerks in rows record the arriving dead
with meticulous kindness, while Eternity
muffles the tapping from ranks of typewriters.

All questions of Life and its years are filed
in the grey reassurance of Ever-after.
Wartime. The uniformed crews arrive companionably,
accepting the issue of wings can wait for another time.
More paperwork, more presentation for the case
of a rose carrying the argument, and Love wins.

And here, clutching drinks, plush-seated
in today's colour-filled, churning world
we know some things are better shared
in our collective lonely dark.

'L'ÉCLISSE'

—Directed by Michelangelo Antonioni, 1962. Italy.

But the scene in the Bourse you say
while I brake flash of red slip
round a cyclist *you must remember
that 8 minutes* and a bus pulls over
no one getting off *as though money
is all there is* not bad early afternoon
schools not out *the woman, the one
in high heels* there's a van loaded
with ladders *you remember her, the flat,
the walk through high rise and concrete*
one of those lorries carrying meat pies
*two lovers talking all night and
the way he uses sound* engine straining
but it's only the bridge *carrying
the narrative but the destination* another
diversion white-lining probably *never
matters then the streets emptied* green light
(good!) *and everything lost—plot people—
you must* watch the lorry they always
run lights *have seen it* and the ambulance
not flashing blue not wailing
don't you remember?

SHOT IN ACADEMY RATIO

—*Ida*, directed by Paweł Pawlikovski, 2013. Poland.

The title's unfamiliar but in the first few frames
I recognise some faces. Not their story, yet
I'm half a beat ahead. I know
she'll light a cigarette and crash the car
(that vodka, a mistake), that there'll be woods
and no one saying much. The past
bulks larger than the present, both
in shades of frozen grey. Someone will die.
I haven't been there but I have, in parallel,
as though watching myself watching
a film in another country and another time.
I wake to see the credits rolling senselessly
like marbles, vowels and consonants
rattling dissonant, helpless to explain.

'IF I'VE GOT TO REMEMBER...'

—Leonard Cohen: 'Tonight will be fine', *Songs from a Room*, 1969

Memory plays vinyl, its needle
tracing the groove and riding light
on the fall, rise, fall of the turntable,

crac-crac of a scratch, the old scar
catching the same return,
making its own record of, one-off,

that place, back then, back when
something careless—dust, or one of us
stumbling, mistaking the moment—

made it, *crac-crac*, permanent
and though there are other ways
to play this song, it's cut into the track,

crac-crac, this version, ours (or mine)
imperfect, pressed and circling,
static crackling like a distant storm.

THE PAINTER OF ICONS

The daily racketty world withdraws,
taking the smells of onions, fish
and ripe apricots into hiding.
Time drains down to the single spot
somewhere below his heart
then vanishes, while brushes wait
cleanly, in a sheen of silence,
prepared for service. A lifetime
condenses into an emptied self,
all the loud company banished,
family gone. His boots
were worn through on the journey
to this: one wooden panel, where today
the trinity of angels will emerge—
seated, the table set, on golden ground—
in conversation. The plateau of the past
spreads out, where he is nothing
and only tradition lives, outlasting
the eyes and hands, sables and paint,
moving the angels into light.

TWO PLANTS

Look, I'm saying *leaf* and already
your mind is playing it. Leaf-ish, leaf-shaped,
leaf-green (whatever that is). No longer
my selfish leaf but the air between us—
leaf-breath, leaf-edged, and fresh
as the season you've chosen for it,
in close-up. Whenever you hear *leaf*
you enter its time: whether
unfurling or falling, or even
straight in the high noon of summer's clock,
or quiet in a wall's untroubled shade,
you've grasped it. My leaf is another matter—
of itself, and turning inwards—but yours
has the sappy spring of the uncoiling year,
new-minted. Or I think it has.

INTO THE SOLSTICE

Up country, into shortening days
where telling time by a shadow's depth
falters. We are caught out
in old habits from the fens
of level hours, and it's not just the valleys
with their tangled topple of trees
and the river's dark twist,
or the scowl of low hedges
and thinning grass. It's not
the gloved and thick-coated light
or how sheep graze the last scrap of sun.
It's more what's beyond, how the earth prunes
what the sky gives, clipping its edges.

Are we ever ready for winter's shrinking,
the counting down? On a lonely farm
ice sits, a sightless skin over a flat roof,
like a black mirror draining the sky.

For someone, life slips sideways
out of the frame, and death
is the old woman mopping the corridors,
name-badge obscured, her face turned away.

PETITION

Let today be ordinary. Just
quiet. Sky unmemorably grey.
Nothing red-letter. Nothing to stain
the future's calendar.

Let it leave no mark or claim,
no darkening of loose skin under the eyes
or tightness round the heart. A day
without a bruise or accident.

Let its business be nothing more
than breath and listening to the the fridge
humming the leftovers to sleep,
the clock moving on the minutes.

Let it end no worse than it started,
only older, only over. Starless.

STONES

Winter lifts them to the surface—
pebbles and knife-edged flints, splinters of quartz—
bright when the fork shakes them loose, the earth
settling back to leave them clean
and obstinate. Last year
cleared the ground ahead of sowing.
This year finds its work undone,
a new month's round of kneeling, sifting,
skimming away under the hedge. Last year
I thought to write this down but summer
shoulders in too fast, too all-at-once
and green, running to seed too soon.
Stones wait; their time is counter-seasonal,
frosted and wordless, patient and ordinary,
world without end and never an amen.

A TRICK OR THE LIGHT

A heart-blink soon corrected
by reason and binoculars—how
the shining figure standing in the yew's
dense dark is nothing, only lately-yellowed leaves
caught in low sun, an unexpected angle.

But there is haunting beyond sight, perhaps
a golden bough such as Aeneas carried
as passport to the speaking dead, or
frost, sun-lifted into drifting breath,
that might be ghost, or revenant, or angel.

'CONSUMIR PREFERENTE ANTES DEL FIN DE:'

The small print's neatly in three languages
but no one filled it in, leaving
the answer open. *Mel de Eucalipto,
Mel de Galicia, Rías Baixas*—
the jar re-used, its label still intact
giving no clue to when or where
one of us (which?) assembled words,
phrase book in hand, and faltered
through the *Por favor* and *Gracias.* No year—
though that could be re-built from journals,
tickets, stuff of travel living on
in guide books growing out of date—
but would it matter? What remains
are streets of pilgrims, tired and radiant
and badged with scallop shells,
then, halfway to the station, this one shop,
left side, the usual windowed bleach and tins,
the proudly local honey

and opposite, a roof caved in by history
no one dare speak, fat ridge tiles, clogs of weeds
bunched in old walls, a nothing of a place.
And yet. The argument of memory goes on
picking up smallness—a neighbouring window
crowded with guitars (electric, gaudy), camellias
in every square (so it was March), their petals
slippery on the stone. Cathedral bells,
the rain, the rain. How careful washing
keeps the label's lustre.
How wonderful the honey was.

SHOPPING LIST

If a poem is a short story
with, as Ted Berrigan says,
the boring bits left out, then what
is this shopping list (one side)
and list of names (reverse)
written in a scrawl so nearly mine
I'm halted?

It's a blink of parallel living; caught,
yes, in a library book I'd borrowed before
but not my list, not in this life. I'd never
cross through single items quite like that.
Someone else is firmer, buys two sorts of milk,
has a blue pen for Ibuprofen.
True, we share a need for coffee and muesli
along with loo and kitchen rolls.
For so short a list it's heavy on paper.
And her list of friends (why assume 'her', this avatar?).
No one here I know, unless—Fiona? Richard?
But they would never appear together like this.
And as for Siegfried—no.
I definitely don't know Siegfried.

THE FOUR OLD THINGS

(Plans to destroy the Four Olds began in Beijing 1966,
as part of the Cultural Revolution.)

Get out, he said, *and take your bags*
from our newly happy State.
We've no use now for your tattered rags
or sentimental debate.

So Customs clutched at his cloak and went
and struggled with laboured breath
and daren't look back at the ages spent
on birth and marriage and death.

And Habits left his daily round
for a barren and stony road
and all ahead was unknown ground
and his heart was a heavy load.

And Culture wept in his threadbare boots
as he staggered away from the past
and from people bereft of their ancient roots
who were shorn of things that would last.

But Thinking, though lamed like a tired mule
worn down and burdened with care,
hung on to a scrap he'd carried from school
when he coughed through the mountain air.

For he knew from the times he'd spent in books
since the earliest days of his youth
that the future is never the same as it looks
when your Leader believes he's Truth

but that Revolutions turn their wheel:
they will find some new-made track.
And by hook or by crook, beg, borrow or steal,
these Four Old Things would come back.

THE PRIZE-WINNING MATHEMATICAL THEORY

'Mathematician [Sir Martin Hairer] wins $3m prize for work on effect of stirring tea'
  —*Guardian* headline, 10/09/20

First things. The kitchen hiss of coffee (and your tea) and being
brave enough for Radio 4 bringing the latest numbers in
and already the day is too much with us. Routine
grinds the smallest ritual. *Make it new, new, new*
whisper shadows, having promises to keep, all
as thoughtless as a teaspoon circling in a teacup

here where there is no formula for fluctuating days
or how time drifts. (Think of the sea; forget it. Too far off.)
The radio talks up sport, such as there is, half-listened-to,
straining for a solution, then segues to an airy half-heard tale
of mathematics. Unlikely, but it shimmers teasingly
beyond the possible, far from the unloved classroom

till I am become as a little child again, cross-legged and wide-eyed
at the edge of knowledge, where numbers are translated
to a sudden paradise—but no, not quite, but yes—
a Xanadu mapped and intricate and lit. I would follow
this pied piper into the mountain, spellbound in the music
of those spheres, their grace, the notes scaling and springing,

joy visible as dance steps while the evolving equation
works itself out, playing those two equals, Random and Order,
around a spoon, stirring tea, a brave new world of Regularity Structures,
tamed and charmed—and now, light touch of a pre-set—
the radio's pulsing and *te-ll-ing the gl-o-ry of G-od*
and what's a heaven for if you can't reach for an answer,
                              this gift, almost graspable.

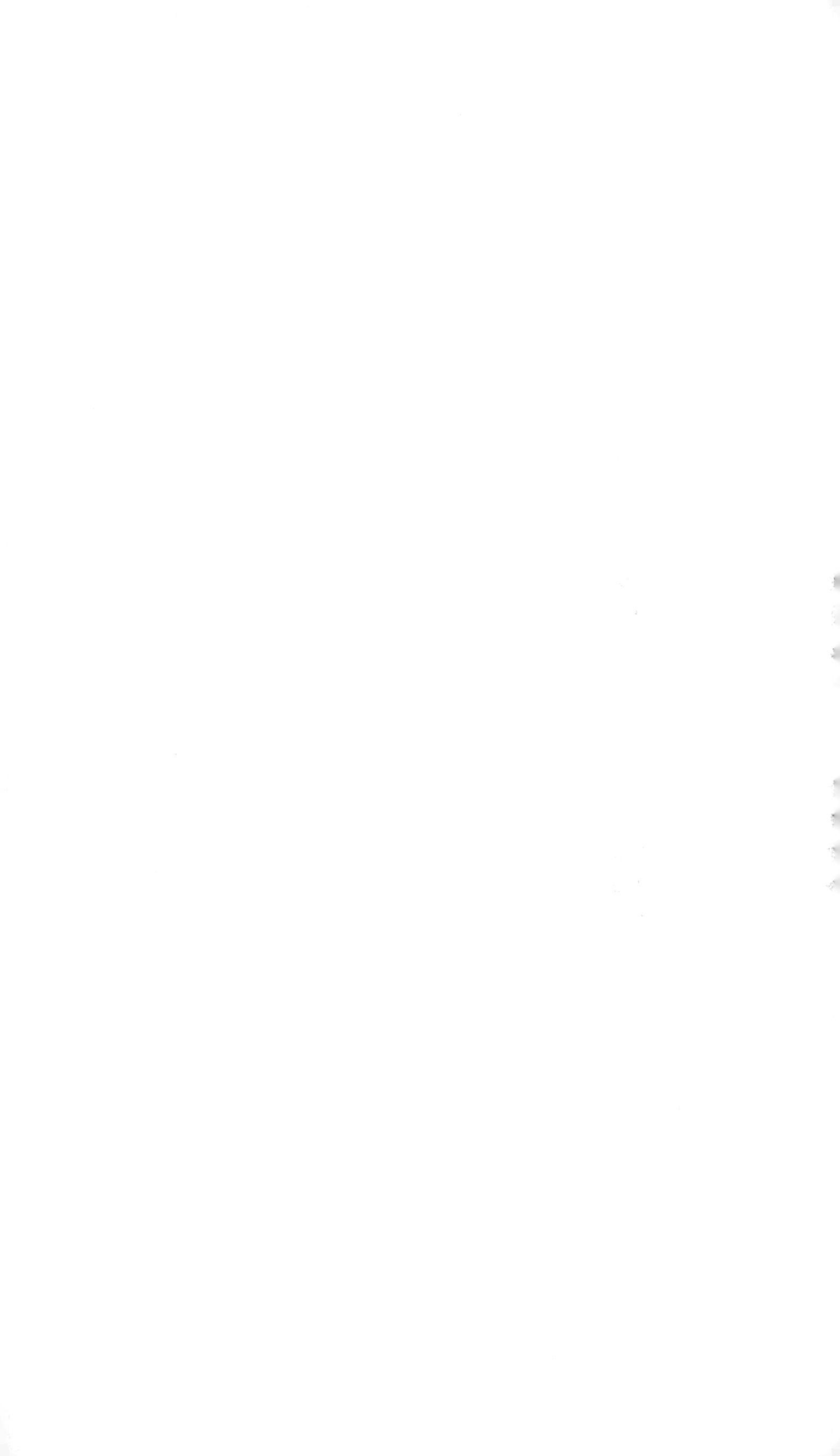

ABOUT THE AUTHOR

D. A. Prince lives in Leicestershire and London. She read English Language and Literature at Reading University, trained as a librarian and subsequently worked in teaching and educational administration. Writing was always a parallel life, with poetry and reviews published in a range of literary magazines. This is her third full collection from Happen*Stance*—the second, *Common Ground*, won the East Midlands Book Award, 2015.